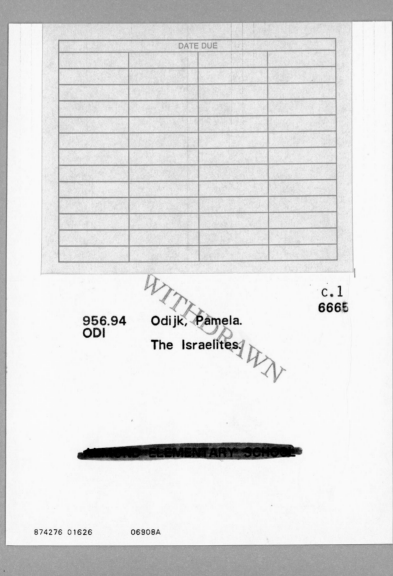

DATE DUE

The Israelites

THE ANCIENT WORLD

The Israelites

Pamela Odijk

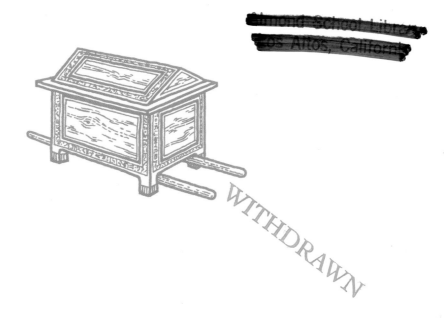

Silver Burdett Press

Acknowledgments

The author and publishers are grateful to the following for permission to reproduce copyright photographs and prints:

ANT/NHPA pp. 14, 15; Coo-ee Historical Picture Library pp. 16, 17, 18, 20, 27, 32; Dale Mann p. 40; The Mansell Collection pp. 11, 21, 25, 28, 34, 39; Mary Evans Picture Library p. 33; Ron Sheridan's Photo-Library pp. 10, 13, 22, 23, 29, 30, 31, 37, 41 and the cover photograph.

While every care has been taken to trace and acknowledge copyright, the publishers tender their apologies for any accidental infringement where copyright has proved untraceable. They would be pleased to come to a suitable arrangement with the rightful owner in each case.

First published 1989 by
THE MACMILLAN COMPANY OF AUSTRALIA PTY LTD
107 Moray Street, South Melbourne 3205
6 Clarke Street, Crows Nest 2065
Associated companies and representatives throughout the world.

American adaption by Rabbi Steven Kushner.

First published in the United States in 1990
by Silver Burdett Press, Englewood Cliffs, N.J.

Printed in Hong Kong

Library of Congress Cataloging-in-Publication Data

Odijk, Pamela, 1942–
    The Israelites / Pamela Odijk
      p.   cm.—(The Ancient world)
    Summary: Explores Jewish life and culture in ancient
Israel.
    1. Jew—Civilization—To 70 A.D.—Juvenile literature.
2. Palestine—Civilization—Juvenile literature. 3. Bible.
O.T.—Antiquities—Juvenile literature. [1. Jews—
Civilization—To 70 A.D. 2. Palestine—Civilization.] I. Title.
II. Series: Odijk, Pamela, 1942—   Ancient world.
DS112.035 1990
956.94'0042924—dc20   89-39620
ISBN 0-382-09888-9   CIP
                               AC

The Israelites

Contents

The Israelites: Timeline

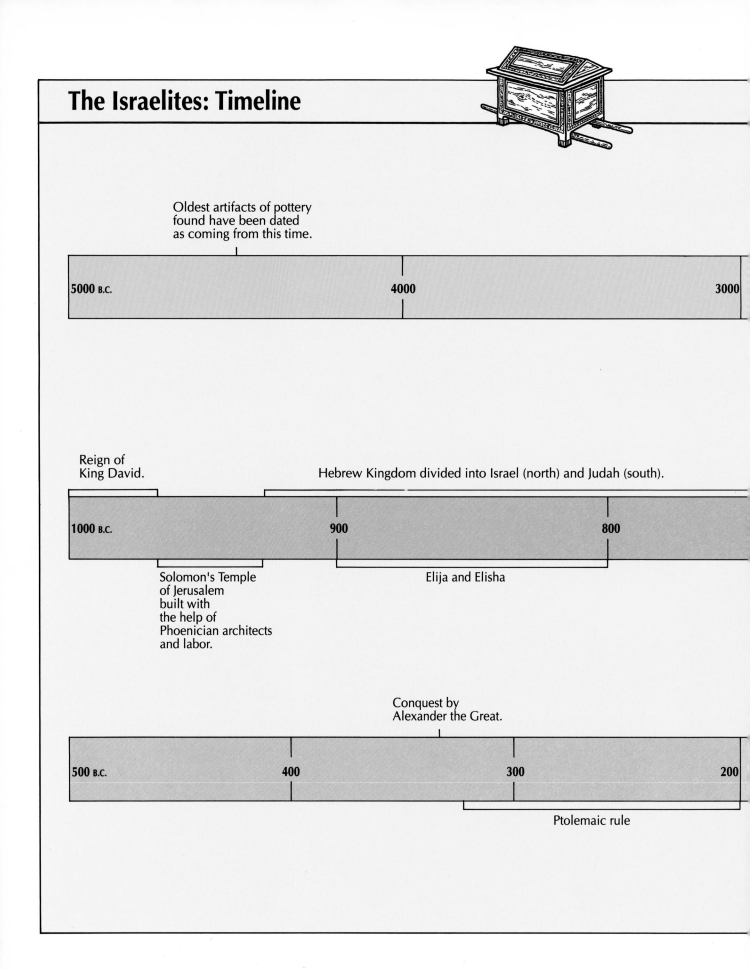

Oldest artifacts of pottery found have been dated as coming from this time.

| 5000 B.C. | | 4000 | | 3000 |

Reign of King David.

Hebrew Kingdom divided into Israel (north) and Judah (south).

| 1000 B.C. | | 900 | | 800 |

Solomon's Temple of Jerusalem built with the help of Phoenician architects and labor.

Elija and Elisha

Conquest by Alexander the Great.

| 500 B.C. | 400 | | 300 | 200 |

Ptolemaic rule

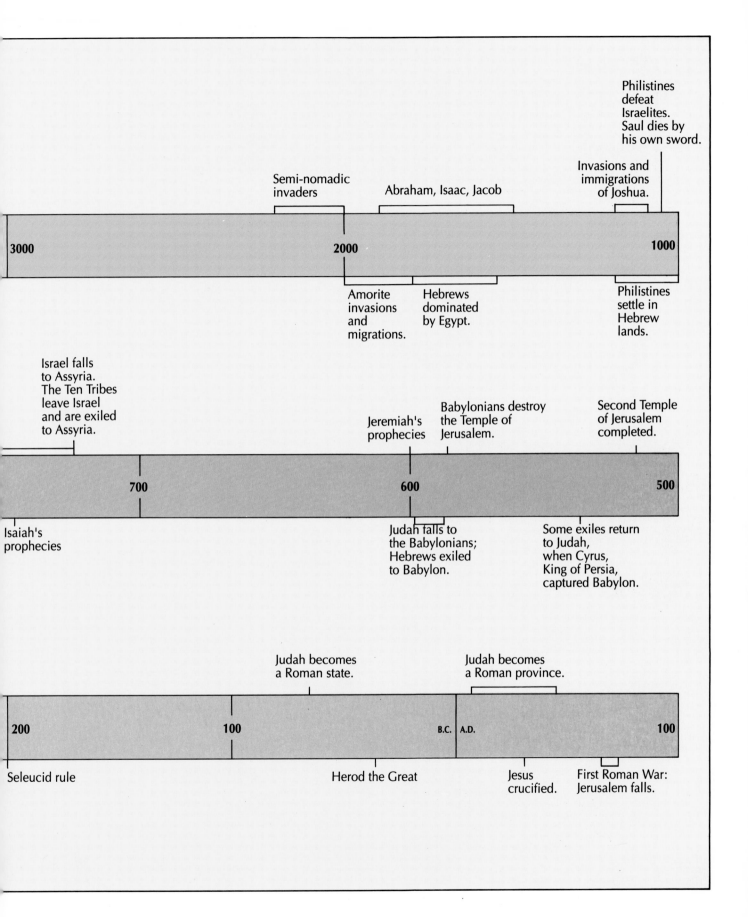

Philistines
defeat
Israelites.
Saul dies by
his own sword.

Semi-nomadic
invaders

Abraham, Isaac, Jacob

Invasions and
immigrations
of Joshua.

3000 **2000** **1000**

Amorite
invasions
and
migrations.

Hebrews
dominated
by Egypt.

Philistines
settle in
Hebrew
lands.

Israel falls
to Assyria.
The Ten Tribes
leave Israel
and are exiled
to Assyria.

Jeremiah's
prophecies

Babylonians destroy
the Temple of
Jerusalem.

Second Temple
of Jerusalem
completed.

700 **600** **500**

Isaiah's
prophecies

Judah falls to
the Babylonians;
Hebrews exiled
to Babylon.

Some exiles return
to Judah,
when Cyrus,
King of Persia,
captured Babylon.

Judah becomes
a Roman state.

Judah becomes
a Roman province.

200 **100** **B.C.** | **A.D.** **100**

Seleucid rule

Herod the Great

Jesus
crucified.

First Roman War:
Jerusalem falls.

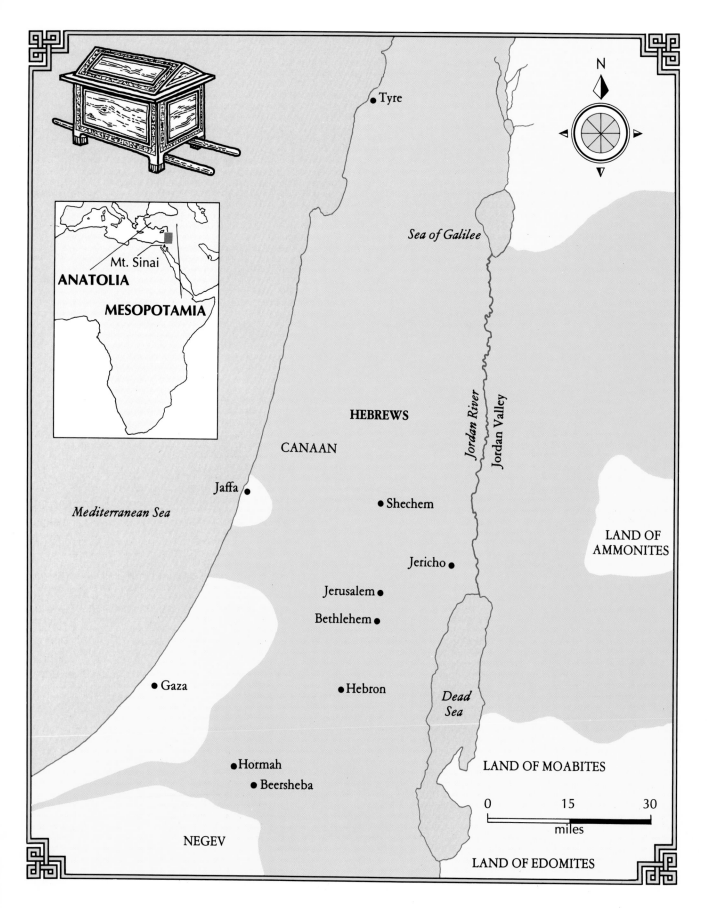

Tyre

Mt. Sinai
ANATOLIA
MESOPOTAMIA

HEBREWS

CANAAN

Jaffa

Mediterranean Sea

Sea of Galilee

Jordan River

Jordan Valley

Shechem

LAND OF
AMMONITES

Jericho

Jerusalem

Bethlehem

Gaza

Hebron

*Dead
Sea*

Hormah

Beersheba

LAND OF MOABITES

| 0 | 15 | 30 |

miles

NEGEV

LAND OF EDOMITES

The Israelites: Introduction

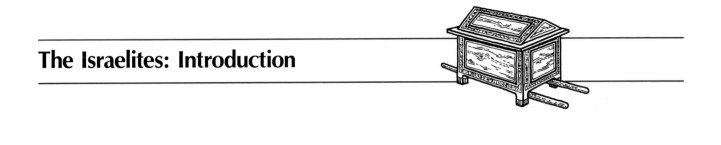

Hebrew Origins

The history of the Israelites is the history of the Jewish people. According to the Hebrew Bible, the Israelites received their name from God: *Yisra-ayl* — meaning "one who struggles with God." Originally, however, the ancestors of the Israelites were known as Hebrews.

Although the origins of the Hebrews are unclear, it is believed that they migrated from **Mesopotamia** to Canaan during the second **millennium** B.C., as their history, place names, and personal names resemble those of Mesopotamia.

On the other hand, the Israelites developed a very clear idea of their beginnings. As recorded in the Hebrew Bible, the Israelites claimed their ancestry from Abraham. Born in the city of Ur in **Sumeria,** Abraham led his family and a large group of followers to Canaan with the belief that they had been "chosen" by God to fulfill some, as yet unstated, special role. In return for their devotion to God, Abraham and his **descendants** would be granted the land of Canaan as an inheritance.

The Hebrew Bible

Almost everything we know about the Israelites is based on information in the Bible. Some people believe the Bible to be completely factual and true. They think that every word in the Bible came directly from God. Other people, however, feel that the Bible is a human product, and that it represents the traditions, remembrances, and beliefs of the Israelite people. They think that at first it was passed on orally and then, many centuries later, was put in writing. In either event, it is hard to know exactly how historically accurate the Bible is. Nevertheless, that it represents the history of this ancient people and gives us a clear understanding of who and what they were is beyond doubt. The Hebrew Bible is the ancient Israelites' "testament" to their origins and destiny.

The Exodus from Egypt

The central event of the Hebrew Bible is the exodus from Egypt. Even though no other records from the ancient world prove that the exodus happened, most scholars agree that it is an event based in history, occurring sometime around 1250 B.C.

According to the Bible, many Hebrews, descendants of Abraham, had gone down into Egypt due to a famine in Canaan. Rather than returning to Canaan, they remained in Egypt for some time. But they never lost their identity as a unique people. This concerned the Pharaoh, the ruler of Egypt. He made life very difficult for them. The Hebrews were made into slaves. Fearing they would multiply, the Pharaoh ordered the killing of all newborn male Hebrews. According to the Hebrew Bible, one child was saved when his mother placed him in a reed basket on the Nile River. That child, to be raised by the daughter of the Pharaoh, would be known by the name of Moses (meaning "drawn from the water" in Egyptian).

Moses led the Hebrews out of Egypt. The exodus was so impressive that the people decided that it should be remembered forever. In fact, one could say that the exodus from Egypt and the time spent in the wilderness of Sinai on the way home to Canaan transformed the Hebrew descendants of Abraham into the people of Israel. According to tradition, it was during this time that they received the **Torah,** the first part of the Hebrew Bible, which served as a constitution with laws binding the people together in a **covenant** (or contract) with their God, Yahweh. This covenant would define the "special role" of the Israelites: to bring God's word to the peoples of the earth.

The Settlement of Canaan

Following Moses' death in the wilderness of Sinai, the newly formed people returned to their **ancestral** homeland of Canaan. Led by Joshua, the people divided themselves into twelve tribes. Each tribe was led and administered by a judge, who was a tribal leader or elder. Over a period of time, however, the people wanted one ruler for the entire nation.

The United Monarchy

For 100 years the twelve tribes were united under a common king. The first king was Saul (1020–1000 B.C.). Although Saul was relatively ineffective, David (1000–961 B.C.) was most successful. He drove the **Philistines** from the land, centralized the capital in Jerusalem, and reigned over the largest and most powerful kingdom in that part of the world. David's son, Solomon (961–922 B.C.) built a beautiful Temple in Jerusalem, but it came at the cost of forced labor and high taxes. Upon his death, civil war broke out and the united monarchy of Saul, David, and Solomon was divided into two smaller kingdoms of Israel in the north and Judah in the south.

Israel and Judah

Because the two kingdoms lay on the crossroads between Asia, Europe, and Africa, Israel and Judah suffered many invasions. They were often subjected to foreign occupation as

Jerusalem from the Mount of Olives.

The passage of the Red Sea. According to the Bible the Red Sea parted to form a path for Moses and the Israelites when they left Egypt.

well as forced **exile** to the homeland of their conquerors.

Of the two kingdoms, Israel in the north was stronger and wealthier. It comprised ten of the original twelve tribes. Its population was also more **assimilated** into the local Canaanitic culture, much to the anger of the prophets, the guardians of the religious tradition. In the year 722 B.C., the northern kingdom of Israel was conquered and destroyed by Assyria.

Meanwhile, the southern kingdom of Judah managed to live in relative harmony with its larger and more powerful neighbors. However, in 586 B.C. the Babylonians, led by Nebuchadnezzar, destroyed Jerusalem, the capital of Judah, and its Temple, and carried the people to Babylon in exile. Thus began the **diaspora,** or dispersion, of the Israelite people.

As slaves in a foreign land they began to write down all their traditions and beliefs that make up the Torah (the Five Books of Moses). Before these books had been passed on orally. It was also in the diaspora that the Biblical religion of the Israelites began the transformation into what is recognized today as Judaism. And it was in the diaspora that the Israelites came to be known as those from Judah, or Jews.

The Jews under Greek and Roman Rule

Not long after Nebuchadnezzar's destruction of Jerusalem, in 538 B.C., Babylon was conquered by Cyrus of Persia. Cyrus let the Jews return to Jerusalem and Judah and rebuild the Temple, although many would continue to live in Babylon, in the diaspora. But the Jews were not completely free under the Persians. Cyrus appointed governors and the people had to pay taxes.

Two hundred years later, in 333 B.C., the Greek leader Alexander the Great conquered the Jewish/Persian **vassal state** as part of his campaign to take over Persia. The Jews surrendered to Alexander, who let them stay in Judah. Alexander wanted the Jewish people to absorb the Greek culture.

In fact, a great many Jews did. In so doing, however, many also drifted away from their own religion. Outraged by those who turned their backs, on Judaism, a group called the Hasmoneans, popularly remembered as the Maccabees, revolted against the Greeks and their Jewish followers and were victorious. The Hasmonean revolution, occurring around 165 B.C., led to the first independent Jewish state in over 400 years. It did not last long.

A century later, moved by internal conflict, the Hasmoneans invited the Romans to help in their struggle. What the Hasmoneans did not plan on was the Romans staying. In 63 B.C. the Romans took control of the Jewish state and renamed it Palestine (after the earlier Philistine occupiers). Within 150 years, the country would be thrown into chaos, the Temple and Jerusalem destroyed for a second time (in 70 A.D.), and the course of Jewish history set for the next two thousand years: a people forced to live in lands not their own. Not until 1948 would the Jews return to reestablish a Jewish state in their ancestral homeland.

The Israelites being led out of Egypt.

The Importance of Landforms and Climate

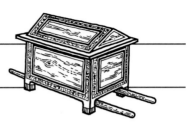

The land of Canaan as settled by the first Hebrews was situated to the south of Anatolia and the west of Mesopotamia between the Mediterranean Sea and the Jordan River. The Jordan River provided a natural barrier separating the Israelites from other people. Fed by the snow of Mount Hermon in the north, the Jordan was the main river flowing into the Sea of Galilee and into the Dead Sea. The Dead Sea is the lowest place below sea level in the world.

The **alluvial** soils on the coastal plain were suitable for agriculture and pastures. The land was covered in places by different kinds of limestone chalk, which allowed the water to seep into natural wells. This water could be brought back to the surface and used for agriculture, and by animals and people during dry times. The valleys of the north had rich and productive soils. To the south is the Negev Desert where the Israelites lived a **nomadic** existence, much in the same way **Bedouin Arabs** do today, tending flocks of sheep, goats, cattle, donkeys, and camels.

Throughout this area the summers are dry with long hot spells, while the winters, when the rains come, are cool. In the south the rainfall is much lower than in the north.

The Jordan valley — site of the first Israelite settlements.

Natural Plants, Animals, and Birds

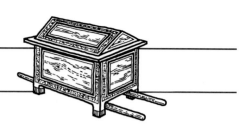

In early times many trees such as the poplar, cedar, ash, cypress, oak, olive, and pine grew there, as well as the date palm and about a thousand species of plants. Some areas in the north were evergreen forests.

Desert scrub grew on sand dunes on the coastal plain and on the Negev Desert in the south.

Animal life in the region included wild boar, wild cats, gazelle, **ibex,** jackals, hyenas, hares, coneys, and badgers. Many species of birds, more of whom were **migratory,** came to these lands. Birds included tropical cuckoos, bustards, sand grouse, and desert larks.

In the desert areas gecko lizards, snakes, vipers, and scorpions lived.

There were also many kinds of fish and insects, and occasionally desert locusts invaded farmlands.

Below: scorpion with young on its back. Scorpions lived in the Negev Desert.

Opposite: the Negev Desert in Israel today.

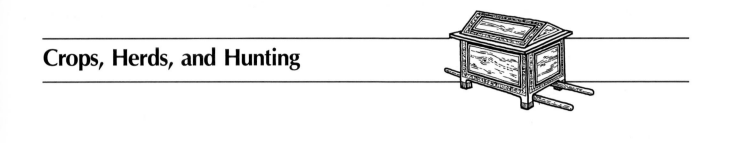

Crops, Herds, and Hunting

Over the ages the Israelites were continually uprooted. Migrations to Egypt during periods of famine and forced exiles by conquering armies left the land barren and uncared for. When the Israelites were able to return to their lands, certain areas, and in particular those in the south, were no longer fertile or able to support settled agriculture.

The Israelites became semi-nomadic herdsmen and, occasionally, farmers. They lived in tents while following their herds of goats and sheep from place to place. When they reached more fertile land in the north, the Israelites settled as farmers and lived in permanent houses. They grew grains and vegetables using simple tools and animal-drawn plows. Dates and nuts were grown in fertile areas, along with grapes, olives, and vegetables.

Fish were also caught to supplement food supplies. Eating the flesh of hunted animals was prohibited by the Israelite religion. Only animals that were herded and slaughtered in a ritual manner could be eaten.

Fishing by the Sea of Galilee. The ancient Israelites fished in the Sea of Galilee.

How Families Lived

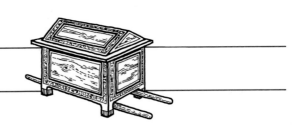

Houses

The nomadic Israelites, residing mainly in Judah, lived in tents and followed their flocks from place to place. The soil was too poor for growing crops, so these wandering Israelites could not establish a permanent settlement. Thus, they remained poor.

The more settled Israelites of the north lived in houses made from sundried bricks. Some of these houses consisted of only one room, while wealthier families could afford larger houses with terraces. Most houses had earth floors that were covered with mats. Furniture consisted of very simple wooden pieces, such as tables, benches, and stools.

Families

Marriage and the family were highly regarded institutions in ancient Israel.

Women washing clothes and fetching water at the Spring of Bittir, as the ancient Israelites once did.

Men

Men were considered the head of the family and had authority over everyone in the family. Men were encouraged to marry and have many children. A man usually paid a price to his bride's father and, in return, the father of the bride gave his daughter a **dowry.** Men could have more than one wife or several **concubines.**

Most men were farmers or herders, but the wealthy also became merchants. Men could be required to become **bondservants** if they were unable to pay their debts, though their children could be sold into slavery as a substitute.

Women

Women were required to obey their fathers before marriage and their husbands after marriage. They were regarded as property belonging to their father or husband. Motherhood was regarded as very important. Women had large families and had to work hard at home. Women cared for the children and did all of the domestic work, including preparing food and making and repairing clothes.

If a woman's husband died, the husband's brother was obliged to marry the woman no matter how many wives he already had, although she had the right to refuse such a marriage. However, a woman was only permitted one husband. Divorce was more easily obtained by men than by women.

Children

Children were expected to obey their parents. Children's lives were modeled almost entirely on the lives of their parents such that they were regarded as substitutes for parents and were expected to acquire all the skills that their parents possessed.

The education of the child, not only in the ways of the world but in the religious tradition, was very important. Initially the responsibility of education lay upon the father but was eventually replaced by a learned elder who was more familiar with the tradition and had the time to teach.

Marriages were arranged for children by their parents as soon as the children reached a marriageable age, often in the teenage years.

Opposite: women crushing olives to extract oil.

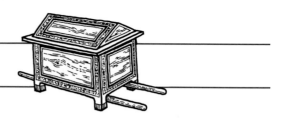

Food and Medicine

Food

The primary diet of the Israelites was fruit, vegetables, dairy, and fish products. Meat was eaten only on special occasions, such as the festivals.

Most fish and animal products were either boiled or roasted for eating. Olive oil was extracted from the fruit of the olive tree and was often used for cooking.

Barley and maize were ground into flour to make bread and cakes. Vegetable gardens provided lentils, chickpeas, cucumbers, garlic, and onions. Fruit such as grapes, figs, dates, olives, pomegranates, and nuts were common.

Food was seasoned with herbs and spices such as nutmeg, dill, cumin, ginger, pepper, saffron, and mint.

Milk, water, wine, and beer were the most common beverages.

Dietary Laws

One of the most distinctive features of the Israelites was their dietary regulations. Only animals with split hooves that chewed their cud, such as lambs and calves, were permissible to eat. They were also required to be without blemish and slaughtered in a particular way.

Only fish with scales and birds that did not feed on other animals could be eaten.

Finally, it was prohibited to cook a baby goat in its mother's milk, a tradition that eventually led to the separation of all milk and meat products in later Judaism.

These laws were known as **kashrut,** meaning "that which is proper."

The first fruits — Israelites gather the harvest of crops including maize and fruit.

Medicine

The religion of the Israelites contained laws or **commandments** that directed daily life. Personal hygiene and public health were covered by these laws.

The Israelites believed in preventive medicine. Their doctors were the first to study the behavior of diseases and how diseases were transmitted. They could then take action against the spread or outbreak of disease.

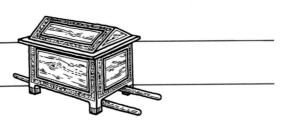

Clothes

Men

In early times Israelite men dressed in simple tunics, sheepskin cloaks, and sandals. As people increased their wealth, they selected richer fabrics from which to make clothing, but the style remained basically the same.

Dress consisted of a shirtlike undergarment of full length. It had sleeves of varying length, plus a rectangular piece of material that could be wrapped around the body. Some men wore more than one shirt, with a shirt made of linen worn next to the skin. They wore low-crowned hats or turban caps. Beards were customary, and the very religious would never cut their side locks or *pe'ot*. These *pe'ot* are believed to be a symbolic reminder of the commandment to leave the corners of one's field for the poor.

It was also customary for men to wear special fringes on the corners of their garments as a reminder of their obligations to God. These fringes were called *tzitzit*.

Women

An Israelite woman would wear a simple draped rectangular garment with a shawl covering her head. Wealthier women wore leather shoes and copied fashion styles from the women of Babylon, Nineveh, Damascus, and Tyre. They also used cosmetics and particularly liked jewelry.

David before the Ark. The ancient Israelites dressed simply, in draped tunics.

Prohibited Dress

The Israelite religion prohibited the mixing of one kind of seed with another. This law extended to the manufacture of clothing. No garment could be made with a combination of woolen and linen fabric.

Israelite law also forbade anyone making marks in the flesh such as tattoos.

Religion and Rituals of the Israelites

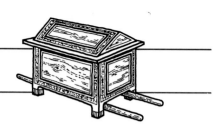

Yahweh

The religion of ancient Israel centered around the worship of Yahweh (sometimes spelled Jehovah). According to the Bible, Moses met Yahweh on Mount Sinai. Unlike the other religions of the time, the God of Israel was not one among many, but the only God of the universe. This belief in only one God is known as **monotheism.** Yahweh was also without body or form, and thus any physical representation of Yahweh such as an idol was strictly forbidden.

Covenant

Central to the worship of Yahweh was the belief that Yahweh and the Israelites had entered into a special relationship with each other. This relationship was known as a covenant. According to the covenant, the Israelites were to follow all the rules and regulations as stated in the Torah (the Five Books of Moses). In return, Yahweh would be the God of Israel,

The tomb of Joseph. Joseph was one of the twelve sons of Jacob, and as such, the leader of one of the twelve tribes of Israel.

promising to protect them, increase their numbers, and give them the land of Canaan as an inheritance forever. The rite of male **circumcision,** performed on the eighth day after birth, was the symbol of the covenant (no such ceremony existed for girls).

The Temple

The primary form of worship in ancient Israel was animal and meal (grain) sacrifice. Although all Israelites were commanded to bring offerings for sacrifice, only those of the tribe of Levi were permitted to participate in the ritual matters of Temple life. Only the **Levites,** those directly descended from Aaron (Moses' brother), could become a priest or **Kohen.** Only the priests were permitted to offer up sacrifices upon the altar.

Originally, sacrifices were not offered in any one central location until David made Jerusalem his capital. From that time until the Roman destruction of the second Temple in A.D. 70, sacrifices were permitted only in Jerusalem. Following David's death, Solomon constructed a large and beautiful Temple in Jerusalem.

The Temple was designed not only as a place in which to offer the sacrifices but as a permanent home for the **Ark of the Covenant.** The Ark, according to tradition, contained the tablets bearing the Ten Commandments that Moses brought down from Mount Sinai.

The Festivals

Although sacrifices were offered daily and on the Sabbath, three times a year all Israelites would come to Jerusalem for festivals: *Pesach,* the springtime festival; *Shavuot,* the celebration of first fruits; and *Sukkot,* the final harvest. In the early autumn Israelites would also come to Jerusalem for their most holy days, *Rosh Hashanah* (the New Year celebration) and *Yom Kippur* (the Day of Atonement).

The Prophetic Tradition

The religion of ancient Israel, however, involved more than sacrificial offerings. A major part of the Torah were laws regulating moral and ethical conduct. The **prophets,** men like Amos and Isaiah and Ezekiel, became the conscience of the people, reminding them that God expected them to behave with goodness and decency.

Religious Life in the Diaspora

Following the destruction of Jerusalem and the exile to Babylon in 586 B.C., the Israelites were forced to adapt their worship to an environment without a Temple. Over the generations, the **synagogue** (place of assembly) arose as an alternative institution for Jewish worship. Similarly, in place of sacrifice, the Jews created an elaborate and beautiful collection of prayers. Following the destruction of the second Temple in A.D. 70, the synagogue and worship through prayer became the standard of Jewish religious life.

Messiah

The Jews developed the concept of a **messiah** while in the diaspora. Messiah, meaning "annointed," originally referred to a king from the line of David who would restore the Israelite monarchy while bringing back all the exiles to Jerusalem. All kings in ancient Israel were annointed. Over the centuries, as the possibility for such **sovereignty** became more remote, the notion of messiah became idealized into a messenger from God who would save the entire world.

Qumran — cave of the Dead Sea Scrolls, where ancient Israelite religious writings have been found.

Obeying the Law

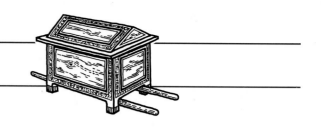

According to the Bible, Moses received the Torah from God on top of Mount Sinai. When he came down from the mountain, Moses gave to Israel the "ten commandments" that had been inscribed upon two tablets of stone. This was not to suggest, however, that there were only ten commandments. In fact, the religion of the Israelites was made up of many commandments, contained in the Torah, directing people how to live their daily lives, as well as how to practice their religion.

Often translated as "Law," the word Torah is best understood as "Teaching." Its purpose was to serve as a guide for living a moral life. The Torah contains laws regulating the treatment of slaves and ethical conduct in war, how one should offer sacrifice, and how one should treat his or her parents. Anyone who was an Israelite was therefore a member of the "covenant" community and required to observe the commandments of the Torah.

The Recording of the Torah

Although tradition has it that the tablets containing the "ten commandments" were safe-kept in the Ark of the Covenant at the Temple in Jerusalem, the majority of the laws and traditions of the Torah were originally passed on orally. Special people memorized the Torah and taught it to the next generation. But following the destruction of Jerusalem and the exile to Babylon in 586 B.C., the leaders of the community decided that the Torah should be written down. Scribes (men specially trained in the art of writing) recorded the Torah on pieces of **parchment** that were then sewn into a large **scroll.** Such scrolls are still used in Judaism today.

In the middle of the fifth century B.C., a scribe called Ezra read to the Jews from scrolls referred to as the "Book of the Law of Moses." For several days the Levites read from these scrolls. The contents of these scrolls were accepted as the laws and traditions that the Jewish people would respect forever. This is the first known instance of a public reading of the Torah.

The Dead Sea Scrolls

The oldest known existing pieces of parchment containing parts of the Hebrew Bible are called the Dead Sea Scrolls. Found in caves near the Dead Sea in 1947, these scrolls were placed in earthen jars two thousand years ago. They had been written by scribes who lived in small, out-of-the-way communities, the most famous of which was Qumran. These scrolls have helped us understand much about ancient Israel.

Opposite: Moses coming down from Mt. Sinai with the Ten Commandments.

24

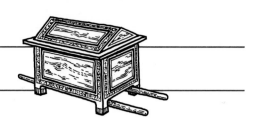

Writing It Down: Recording Things

In early times the Hebrews learned to write in **cuneiform** writing. This was done on wet clay tablets with a wedge-shaped **stylus.** Later the Hebrews began to write on **papyrus,** parchment, and fragments of broken pottery. This kind of writing was done with a reed pen dipped in ink.

The Hebrew alphabet was strongly influenced by the alphabets of the Canaanites and Phoenicians. There are two Hebrew alphabets, the early Hebrew and the Classical or Square Hebrew. The original Hebrew alphabet was created over 3,500 years ago and had twenty-seven signs. These signs, or pictographs, were similar to the **hieroglyphics** of ancient Egypt.

Between the sixth and second centuries B.C., the Square Hebrew alphabet became more commonly used. It contained twenty-two letters, indicating a change from a language of pictures to one of words made up of letters. Over the next 1,500 years, this alphabet developed into the modern Hebrew alphabet. Hebrew is read from right to left.

Several hundred ancient Hebrew inscriptions exist. The oldest example of early Hebrew writing is the Gezer calendar, which dates from the tenth century B.C. Archaeologists have also discovered some scribbling done by a child at Lachish, which included the first five letters of the Hebrew alphabet written in order. This discovery probably indicates that children were taught the alphabet this way.

Weights and Measures

The Israelite system of weights and measures was derived from the Egyptians and Babylonians. The basic units were the *talent,* the *mina,* and the *shekel:*

    a sacred *mina* = 60 *shekels*
    a sacred *talent* = 3,000 *shekels* or 50 sacred *minas*

The measure of volume is thought to have been based on a *bat* = .6 pint (0.37 liter), a *log* = slightly more than .8 pint (½ liter), a *hin* = slightly more than 11 pints (6 liters). Liquid and dry measures were almost the same:

    a liquid *kor* = a dry *homer*
    a liquid *bat* = a dry *efa*

Calendar

Most scholars today trace the calendar of ancient Israel to the Canaanitic calendar. A **lunar** calendar is made up of twelve months and is based on the cycles of the moon. It followed the agricultural seasons of planting, first fruits, and final harvest. The first month of the Israelite calendar fell in the springtime. This calendar is still used by Jews today.

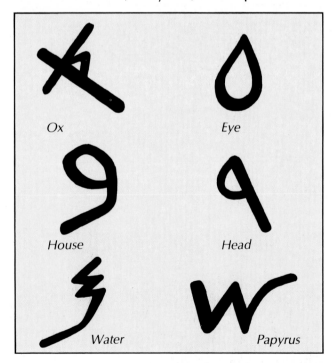

Ox   Eye
House   Head
Water   Papyrus

The early Hebrew alphabet, circa 700 B.C.

Israelite Legends and Literature

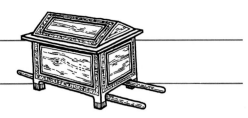

The Hebrew Bible is the largest and most varied collection of literature from the ancient world. It represents nearly two thousand years of writings, ranging from stories to law codes to collections of poetry and prose. Written almost entirely in Hebrew, it reflects many different styles and authors.

The Hebrew language is divided into three periods:

Biblical or Classical Hebrew	In which most of the Hebrew Bible was written.
Mishnaic or Rabbinic Hebrew	The language of the Mishnah or Oral tradition (c. A.D. 200).
Modern Hebrew	The language of the modern-day state of Israel.

Literature of the Hebrew Bible

The Hebrew Bible is composed of three major sections.

The first section of the Hebrew Bible is the Torah. The Torah contains the legends of the first Hebrews, the tradition of the exodus from Egypt, and the many laws and teachings that make up the covenant between Yahweh and Israel.

The Prophets is the second section of the Hebrew Bible. It contains the history of the Israelites from the settlement period to the destruction of Jerusalem by the Babylonians. It is also filled with the poetic and powerful teachings of the prophets.

The Writings is the last part of the Hebrew Bible. It is made up of wise sayings, poetry, and philosophical texts.

Daniel in the Den of Lions, a story from the Bible.

Books of the Hebrew Bible

Torah:
Genesis
Exodus
Leviticus
Numbers
Deuteronomy

Prophets:
Joshua
Judges
Samuel (1 and 2)
Kings (1 and 2)
Isaiah
Jeremiah
Ezekiel
Hosea
Joel
Amos
Obadiah
Jonah
Micah
Nahum
Habakkuk
Zephaniah
Haggai
Zechariah
Malachi

Writings:
Psalms
Proverbs
Job
Song of Songs
Ruth
Lamentations
Ecclesiastes
Esther
Daniel
Ezra-Nehemiah
Chronicles (1 and 2)

Stories of the Bible

There can be no doubt that many of the stories in the Hebrew Bible do not represent actual historical events. Nor is it clear that the authors intended for those stories to be believed literally. They were often meant to teach a lesson. Legends such as Abraham's binding of Isaac taught of faith, while the story of the Golden Calf was a reminder of how easy it was to lose faith.

Many of the Bible's stories were, in fact, borrowed from other cultures. Some were stories that explained how things came to be. The Creation myth and the Flood and even that of Moses in the reed basket have parallels in the literature of Egypt and Mesopotamia. Each of these stories, however, was adapted to reflect the monotheistic beliefs of the Israelites.

The Pharaoh's daughter found Moses in the bulrushes.

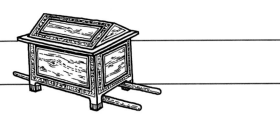

Art and Architecture

Art

The religion of ancient Israel specifically forbade the making of idols. As such, the Israelites left behind no sculpture.

Although art in pictures does not seem to have been common, decorated pottery and jewelry indicate that the Israelites were artistic.

Architecture

In architecture the Israelites borrowed both ideas and craftsmen from Egypt, Phoenicia, Damascus, and Assyria.

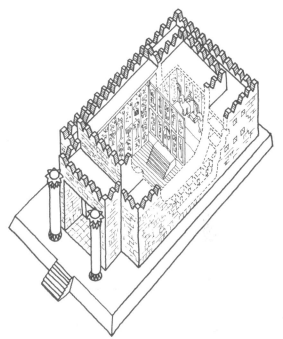

Right: the Temple of Solomon had a porch with pillars on either side, a sanctuary, and an inner sanctum where the Ark of the Covenant was kept. Below: the Tower of David, King of Israel 1000-961 B.C.

The Temple of Solomon

King David had planned to build a temple to house the Ark of the Covenant, but this was not done until after his death, during the reign of his son, Solomon.

The ground plan of the Temple of Solomon shows a porch with pillars on either side, a sanctuary, and an inner sanctum, where the Ark of the Covenant was kept. It was built for Solomon by Phoenician craftsmen but with forced laborers. The Temple also contained ideas from Assyrian and Babylonian architecture.

The Temple was believed to have been very lavish. It had much gold with precious stones set as decoration. The doors and walls were paneled with carved cedar and olive wood, and it was considered to have been one of the most beautiful structures of the ancient world. Solomon's Temple was destroyed by the Babylonians in 586 B.C.

The Temple — the most beautiful architectural building in ancient Israel, built first in the tenth century B.C., destroyed and then rebuilt in the sixth century B.C., and finally destroyed in A.D. 70. This is a model of the Temple near Jerusalem today.

Going Places: Transportation, Exploration, and Communication

The Israelites' primary mode of transportation was usually on foot with the occasional use of beasts of burden, such as the ass or horse or camel. The chariot may have been used for rapid transit by the wealthy, but it was mainly used in warfare. The wagon was used for the transportation of heavy items.

Sea travel seems to have been fairly extensive in ancient Israel. We do not know much about the kinds of ships that existed, but we do know that King Solomon had a large fleet of trading vessels.

Following the Babylonian exile, a sophisticated system of signal fires between Jerusalem and Babylon was devised to communicate when the Jewish holy days were to be observed. Most long-distance communication, however, was achieved by messenger or letter. Letters were often written on pieces of parchment, papyrus, or fragments of broken pottery, or inscribed on clay tablets.

Descent upon the Valley of Jordan, where the ancient Israelites once wandered and settled.

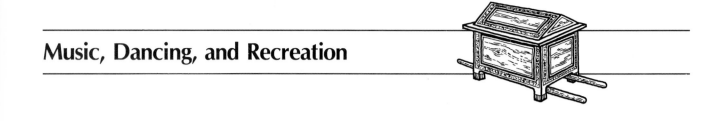

Music, Dancing, and Recreation

The ancient Israelites performed dances as part of their worship, such as those performed before the Ark, in praise of God, and at festivals of thanksgiving. Music and singing accompanied this dancing. Instruments played included the timbrel, the lyre, the tamborine, and a kind of trumpet called the **shofar.**

Much of the singing and music was performed by the Levites. Although we do not know what the melodies sounded like, we do have many of the words of their songs. They are contained in the Book of Psalms.

Leisure must have been important in ancient Israel. Storytelling was entertaining as well as a way to pass on the sacred traditions. There is evidence of board games played with dice.

Hunting for food or game was uncommon among the Israelites.

Psalm 150

Halleluyah.
Praise God in His sanctuary;
　Praise Him in the sky, His stronghold.
Praise Him for His mighty acts;
　Praise Him for His exceeding greatness.
Praise Him with blasts of the horn;

Praise Him with harp and lyre.
Praise Him with timbrel and dance;
　Praise Him with lute and pipe.
Praise Him with resounding cymbals;
　Praise Him with loud-clashing cymbals.
Let all that breathes praise the Lord.
　Halleluyah.

The Feast of Sukkot— a view of the inner porch altar. This festival was to remind people of how the Israelites, after fleeing Egypt, wandered in the desert for forty years before finding their promised land.

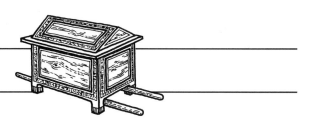

Wars and Battles

The nomadic Israelites had no established armies, armor, or siege weapons for battering down city walls. They were more interested in survival than attack. However, the Israelites did need to defend themselves from invaders. They built walled cities for protection. Their warriors carried weapons such as spears, swords, bows and arrows, and slings. Soldiers were known to have carried shields, but we have no evidence that they wore helmets.

The Assyrians invaded the northern kingdom of Israel in 722 B.C., and for the next century struggled with the southern kingdom of Judah.

Occasionally, some tribes would join together to fight a common enemy, but it was not until the tribes gave way to the united monarchy that the Israelites were able to establish a standing army. King Saul (1020–1000 B.C.) attempted to unify the twelve tribes. He did assemble and lead an army, but his army could not hold back the fierce Philistines and was seriously defeated. When this happened, Saul died by his own sword.

King David (1000–961 B.C.) was one of Saul's armed men. He understood the importance of possessing a strongly walled city and decided to try to capture a fortress held by the Canaanites on the hill of Jerusalem. His army successfully captured the fortress and David ruled from Jerusalem as the King of all Israel. By the time of his death, David's empire extended well to the north and east into Mesopotamia.

After David, King Solomon (961–922 B.C.) reigned. Although it was a time of peace, Solomon became rich and extravagant and began taxing the Israelites heavily in order to pay his huge debts. This created discontent. When Solomon died the people were divided into the two hostile kingdoms of Israel in the north and Judah in the south.

The Assyrians, under Sargon II, invaded the northern kingdom of Israel in 722 B.C., destroying the kingdom and dispersing the people. The Assyrians then continued a struggle with the southern kingdom of Judah for over a century. Jerusalem looked as if it would be finally taken when the Assyrian army was suddenly weakened by diseases and forced to return home.

The Babylonians then invaded Judah and in 586 B.C. destroyed Jerusalem and exiled the survivors to Babylon. Not for another 400 years, during the Maccabean rebellion of the second century B.C., would the Jews know any form of military strength.

Below: Solomon taxed the Israelites heavily during his reign.

Opposite: the Hanging Gardens of Babylon. After the Babylonians captured Judah in 586 B.C., the Israelites were exiled to Babylon.

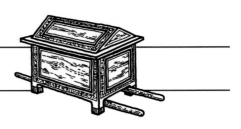

Israelite Inventions and Special Skills

Monotheism

The idea that there was only one God was first introduced by the Israelites. There were some civilizations that developed the belief in gods who were the most powerful, above all other gods. But no one had ever suggested that only one God existed. Yahweh was all-powerful, the creator of the universe.

Even more unique was the notion that Yahweh was without body and was invisible. This idea was completely unheard of before.

The Israelite monotheism was also different because Yahweh was an ethical God. Yahweh's prime concern was the ethical and moral behavior of humanity.

All of these aspects combined to reshape the nature of religion in the western world.

Ethics and Morality

Although all ancient peoples must have developed values for proper conduct within their societies, the Israelites were the first to require moral behavior as an important part of religious life. Laws commanding children not merely to obey but to "honor" their mothers and fathers made the Israelite tradition unique. The Holiness Code of Leviticus, Chapter 19, commands the Israelites "not to insult the deaf nor place a stumbling block before the blind."

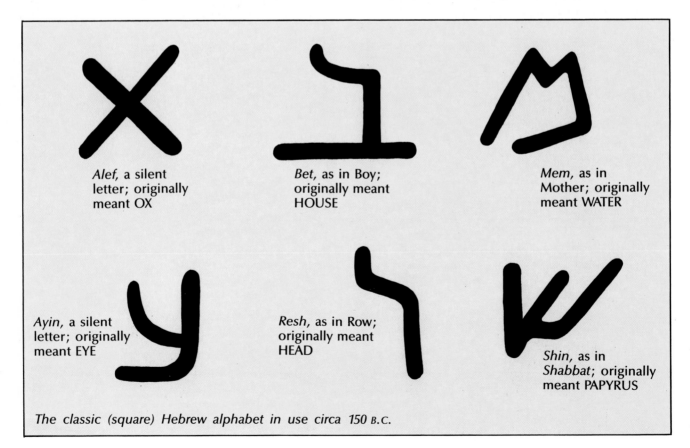

Alef, a silent letter; originally meant OX

Bet, as in Boy; originally meant HOUSE

Mem, as in Mother; originally meant WATER

Ayin, a silent letter; originally meant EYE

Resh, as in Row; originally meant HEAD

Shin, as in *Shabbat*; originally meant PAPYRUS

The classic (square) Hebrew alphabet in use circa 150 B.C.

Copper smelting hearth, King Solomon's mines. The Hebrews experienced the most prosperity under Solomon.

It also commands that "You shall love your neighbor as yourself."

The concept of justice was central to the Israelite religion. Every fifty years all lands were to return to their original owners. All slaves were to be given their freedom. To the Israelites, fair treatment of slaves as well as strangers within the community was important, because the Israelites had been "strangers in Egypt."

This tradition of moral and ethical conduct became the primary message of the prophets, such as that of Amos, "Let justice roll down like waters and righteousness as a mighty stream." Its value would also be shared by the two other major western religions to which Judaism gave rise, Christianity and Islam.

The Sabbath

One of the most enduring Israelite contributions to western civilization was the **Shabbat** or Sabbath day. Although the idea of a day of rest seems to have existed in Mesopotamia, the Israelites were the ones to make it a day devoted to God and holy matters. All forms of work were prohibited on the Sabbath. The ancient Israelites, as the modern-day Jews, observed the *Shabbat* from sunset on Friday to nightfall the following day. Most Christians observe the Sabbath on Sunday.

The Hebrew Alphabet

The Israelites developed their own alphabet and system of writing. They were then able to write on papyrus and parchment, instead of cumbersome clay tablets. This made it much easier to record ideas and stories or events of importance in a brief period of time.

The Hebrew language also transformed its alphabet, which originated in Canaan, from picture symbols to letters in order to form words rather than the Mesopotamian cuneiforms or the Egyptian hieroglyphics. Specially trained scribes, who were often priests, were the first to develop the art of writing in ancient Israel.

Recording the Torah on parchment.

Why the Civilization Declined

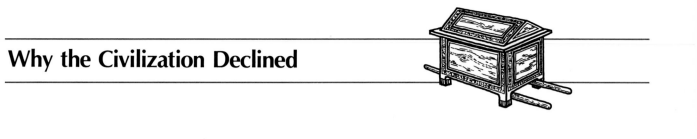

When the Romans destroyed Jerusalem and the Temple in A.D. 70, one might think that the people of Israel would cease to be. Driven from their land, unable to practice their religion in the ways of their ancestors, the Israelites could have easily died out. But they did not.

Jerusalem — last remains of the Temple.

The Jews refused to abandon their identity as a "chosen" people. Their mission of being a "light unto the nations," of spreading the moral and ethical message of Yahweh, had not yet been fulfilled.

Their devotion to God and the covenant was strong. Instead of a single Temple where all Jews would worship, the synagogue made it possible for Jews, wherever they were, to gather together as a community. Without sacrifices, the Jews developed prayers that they could offer to God. Most important, the Jews turned inward toward their most sacred possession, the Torah.

For the next two thousand years the Jewish people committed themselves to the study of Torah. The goal of such study was to determine what the Torah really meant and to understand what God really expected of them. Special teachers of Torah, or **rabbis,** became the leaders of the community. The study and interpretation of Torah became the essence of Jewish life.

No doubt a modern Jew and Abraham would have difficulty recognizing each other. Much has changed in Judaism since the days of ancient Israel. But certain things remain the same. Today's Jews continue to worship Yahweh, although they now pronounce that name *Adonai,* meaning "Lord." The Biblical Sabbath and festivals are still the basis of observance within the religious community. So, too, the ethical and moral teachings continue to have great importance. Today's Jews are still attached to their ancient homeland and traditions. But above all, the Torah is the foundation of Judaism as it was for Moses and the Israelites 3,000 years ago.

Above: the descendants of the ancient Israelites are today's Jews. A Jewish family lighting Sabbath candles at sunset on Friday.

Opposite: the wilderness of Sinai. The Israelites journeyed through this barren wasteland from Egypt to Canaan.

Glossary

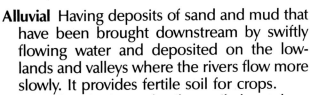

Alluvial Having deposits of sand and mud that have been brought downstream by swiftly flowing water and deposited on the lowlands and valleys where the rivers flow more slowly. It provides fertile soil for crops.

Ancestral Referring to family or tribal members from earlier generations; ancestors.

Ark of the Covenant A gold-plated wooden chest that, according to the Bible, contained the tablets bearing the Ten Commandments.

Assimilated Becoming like the people in whose land you live, often at the cost of your own national or ethnic identity.

Bedouin Arabs Tribes of migrant Arabs who move from place to place with their flocks and herds.

Bondservant A person bound to serve another without being paid wages.

Circumcision The surgical removal of the male's foreskin, in Judaism performed on the eighth day following birth.

Commandment A law or religious obligation.

Concubines Extra women who lived as wives without being officially married to the man with whom they lived.

Coney A small animal similar to a rabbit.

Covenant A contract or agreement between two parties.

Cuneiform An early system of writing done on soft clay tablets with a wedge-shaped stylus.

Descendants Members of a family or tribe who will be born in future generations.

Diaspora From the Greek meaning "the dispersion"; specifically the scattering of the Jews among the nations.

Dowry Money or goods given to the husband from the bride's father at the time of marriage.

Exile To be separated or sent away for a long time from one's country or home.

Hieroglyphics A language with picture symbols instead of words, particularly used by the ancient Egyptians.

Ibex A wild goat with large curved horns. Some shofars are made from ibex horns.

Kashrut The Jewish dietary laws that date back to ancient Israel; kosher food.

Kohen A priest; a direct descendant of Aaron, Moses' brother, from the tribe of Levi.

Levite Of the tribe of Levi; those who ministered within the Temple.

Lunar Referring to the moon; a lunar calendar is based on the cycles of the moon.

Mesopotamia An area of land in western Asia, northwest of the Persian Gulf and southeast of Anatolia.

Messiah Annointed; a king in ancient Israel, later to be thought of as a savior sent from God.

Migratory To pass periodically from one region or climate to another.

Millennium A period of one thousand years.

Monotheism The belief in one God.

Nomadic Pertaining to nomads, a people or tribe that has no permanent home but moves about from place to place.

Papyrus A form of paper made from the fiber of the stem of the papyrus reed that grew in the Nile River valley in Egypt.

Parchment Animal skin that is cleaned, stretched, and dried for use as a material on which to write.

Philistines Also known as the Sea Peoples, a group of warriors who invaded Canaan just prior to the Israelite settlement of that land, and were a feared enemy of the tribes of ancient Israel.

Prophet Inspired leaders in ancient Israel who tried to remind the people of their responsibilities as members of the covenant community.

Rabbi One who is versed in the Torah; a leader of the Jewish community following the destruction of the Temple in A.D. 70.

Scroll Several pieces of parchment sewn together; an early type of book.

Shabbat The Sabbath; a day of complete rest devoted to thoughts of God and holy matters.

Shofar A type of trumpet usually made from a ram or ibex horn.

Sovereignty The state of having independent power or authority in government; being able to rule oneself.

Stylus A pointed or wedge-shaped stick used for making impressions on wet clay tablets.

Sumeria A kingdom in southern Mesopotamia; one of the earliest places of the beginnings of civilization.

Synagogue A place of assembly and prayer that eventually replaced the Temple as the institution of Jewish worship.

Torah The Pentateuch or Five Books of Moses that, according to tradition, was given to Moses on top of Mount Sinai. To this day, the Torah is written in Hebrew on scrolls of parchment and ceremonially read within the synagogue.

Vassal state A state or nation that is dependent upon another state or nation.

The Israelites: Some Famous People and Places

ABRAHAM

Abraham was the first Hebrew. He was born in Mesopotamia and migrated with his wife, Sarah, to the land of Canaan. Although he and his family remained migrants, moving frequently between Canaan, Mesopotamia, and Egypt, Abraham considered Canaan his home.

According to the Bible, Abraham had one son, Ishmael, by Sarah's maidservant Hagar. He later had a legitimate son, Isaac, by his wife, Sarah. As the founder of this people, Abraham is known as the first patriarch, or ancestral father. His son, Isaac, and grandson, Jacob, are also referred to as patriarchs.

JACOB

Jacob was the grandson of Abraham. His name was later changed to Israel, after whom all Israelites or Jews are named. Jacob had two wives, Leah and Rachel. From his wives and their maidservants, he fathered twelve sons. According to the Bible, the descendants of those sons became the twelve tribes of Israel. Jacob had one daughter, Dinah.

THE TWELVE TRIBES OF ISRAEL

The ancient Israelites had first organized themselves into a nation of twelve separate tribes. These tribes claimed descendancy from the sons of Jacob: Reuben, Simeon, Levi, Judah, Dan, Naphtali, Gad, Asher, Issachar, Zebulun, Joseph, and Benjamin. Each of the tribes settled separate portions of the land of Canaan. The tribe of Levi did not receive land because they were responsible for working within the Temple in Jerusalem. The two sons of Joseph, Manasseh and Ephraim, each received tribal lands on behalf of their father, thus completing the twelve tribal settlements.

Following the death of Solomon, the united monarchy broke into two separate kingdoms. The northern kingdom of Israel was made up of ten tribes: Reuben, Simeon, Dan, Naphtali, Gad, Asher, Issachar, Zebulun, Manasseh, and Ephraim. In 722 B.C. Israel was destroyed by Assyria. We do not know what happened to these ten "lost" tribes.

The southern kingdom of Judah was comprised of the tribes of Judah, Benjamin, and the Levites who lived within the Temple in Jerusalem. The Jewish people would be formed from these last three tribes.

MOSES

Moses was the leader of the Israelites in their exodus from Egypt. According to the Bible, he was born to a Hebrew mother but was placed in a reed basket upon the Nile to spare him certain death at the hands of the Egyptians. Found by the daughter of the Pharaoh, Moses was raised as an Egyptian.

Upon discovering his true identity, Moses rose up to lead the Israelites from Egypt to the wilderness of Sinai where, according to the Bible, he received the Torah from God and then gave it to Israel.

A man of extraordinary leadership and profound humility, Jewish tradition considers Moses the greatest prophet of all time.

DAVID

David was the second king of the united monarchy. During his reign the ancient Israelites enjoyed their greatest political and military strength. His kingdom extended well into Mesopotamia. He centralized the government in Jerusalem and established a dynasty that is still regarded as the greatest in Jewish history.

David began his career in the court of King Saul as a musician and singer. Many of the Psalms are believed to have been composed by David. He was a charismatic leader who united the entire nation under his rule. The prophets believed that the messiah would be descended from King David.

SOLOMON

A son of King David, Solomon became king upon his father's death. According to tradition, Solomon was very wise. He is said to have authored many of the Proverbs as well as the Book of Ecclesiastes and the Song of Songs. The Bible suggests that Solomon had hundreds of wives and concubines, many of whom were to form political alliances.

Solomon's greatest accomplishment was the construction of a large and beautiful Temple in Jerusalem. Often regarded as the most impressive building in the ancient Near East at that time, Solomon's Temple was destroyed by the Babylonians in 586 B.C.

JERUSALEM

Jerusalem is situated in today's Judean hills, midway between the Dead Sea and the Mediterranean Sea. Originally it was a Canaanitic city, with a history that dates back into prehistoric times.

Jerusalem took on its importance when David established his capital there. It later became the site of both the first and second Temples.

Because of its location in the center of ancient Israel, Jerusalem became the dividing line between the two kingdoms of Israel and Judah. Jerusalem was actually located within the tribal boundaries of Benjamin.

Over the centuries Jerusalem was conquered many times. This is evidenced by the many different styles of foreign architecture that have survived there. To this day, Jerusalem is regarded as a holy city by all three monotheistic religions, Judaism, Christianity, and Islam.

JEREMIAH

Jeremiah was a prophet and reformer in the southern kingdom of Judah. He lived in the latter half of the seventh century B.C., during a period of social and religious unrest. Jeremiah predicted that unless the people changed their ways, Jerusalem and the Temple would be destroyed. For this he was thrown into prison. Although he was allowed to go free, Jeremiah would eventually seek refuge in Egypt just prior to the destruction of Jerusalem by the Babylonians.

Tradition suggests that, in addition to the Book of Jeremiah, he authored the Book of Lamentations.

EZEKIEL

Ezekiel was one of the most dramatic prophets of ancient Israel. Born into a priestly family, Ezekiel witnessed the destruction of Jerusalem and the exile to Babylon in the sixth century B.C.

Although he foresaw the coming of the destruction, his prophecies are often filled with messages of comfort and consolation. His most famous vision is that of the Valley of Dry Bones, a prediction of the resurrection of those who died during the destruction of Jerusalem.

Most of his writings were intended for the exiles living in Babylon. They are contained in the Book of Ezekiel.

Index

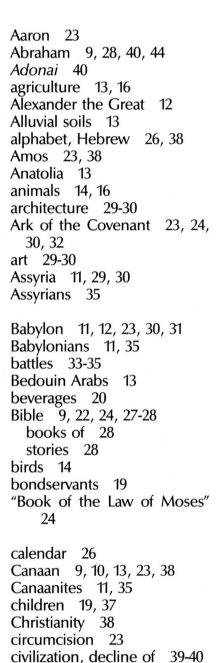

Mediterranean Sea 13
men 19, 21
Mesopotamia 9, 13, 28, 35, 38
messiah 23
monotheism 22, 28, 36
morality 36-38
Moses 9, 10, 22, 23, 24, 28, 40, 44
motherhood 19
Mount Hermon 13
Mount Sinai. *See* Sinai
music 32

Nebuchadnezzar, King 11, 12
Negev Desert 13
nomadic existence 13, 17

origins 9

Palestine 12
papyrus 26, 31, 36, 38
parchment 31, 38
parents, honoring 19, 37
pe'ot 21
Persians 12
Pesach 23
Pharaoh 9
Philistines 10, 35
Phoenicia 29
plants 14

priests 23, 38
prohibited dress 21
prophets 23, 38, 45
Prophets (section of the Bible) 27-28
Psalms 32

Qumran 24

rabbis 40
recreation 32
religion 22-23
    see also Torah
rituals 22-23
Roman rule 12, 39
Rosh Hashanah 23

Sabbath 23, 38, 40
sacrifices 23
Sargon II, King 35
Saul, King 10, 35
scribes 24, 38
Sea of Galilee 13
Shabbat. See Sabbath
Shavuot 23
shofar 32
Sinai 9, 10, 22, 23
slaves 9, 24, 37
Solomon, King 10, 23, 30, 31, 35, 45

spices 20
Stylus 26
Sukkot 23
Sumeria 9
synagogue 23, 40

tattoos 21
taxation 35
Temple in Jerusalem 10, 11, 12, 23, 24, 30, 39, 40
Ten Commandments 23, 24
Torah 10, 11, 22, 23, 24, 27, 40
transportation 31
trees 14
twelve tribes of Israel 10, 44
tzitzit 21

vassal state 12
vegetables 20

wars 24, 33-35
weights 2
women 19, 21
Writings (section of the Bible) 27

Yahweh. *See* God
Yom Kippur 23